PRODUCT INFORMATION:

Besides *Noah*, Mary Rice Hopkins has also published the popular children's books *Hip, Hip, Hip, Hippopotamus* and *Animal Alphabet*.

However, Mary is best known for her creative ministry in children's music. Mary writes and performs songs with a special message for children of all ages. Her songs help kids and adults alike understand who God is and how much He loves them, put into practice the principles of sharing and caring, and realize how valuable they are in the eyes of their Creator.

For a copy of the recorded song "Noah Was a Faithful Man" or to receive more information about Mary's cassettes, CDs, videos or songbooks you can write or call:

MARY RICE HOPKINS
PO Box 362
Montrose, CA 91021

(818) 790-5805   FAX (818) 790-9756   FOR ORDERS ONLY 1-800-274-8674

email: Bigsteps@aol.com   www.maryricehopkins.com

To see more of Wendy Francisco's art visit her website:

www.wendyfrancisco.com

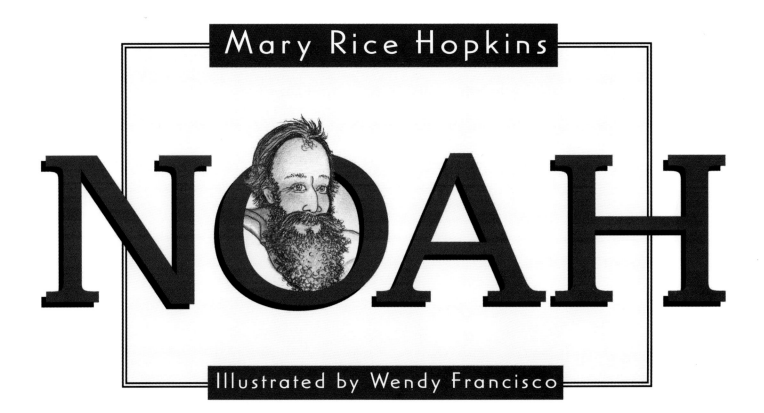

Mary Rice Hopkins

NOAH

Illustrated by Wendy Francisco

CROSSWAY BOOKS • WHEATON, ILLINOIS
A DIVISION OF GOOD NEWS PUBLISHERS

AUTHOR AND ARTIST DEDICATION

To our husbands, Gary Hopkins and Don Francisco.

The faithful men in our lives.

Noah

Copyright © 1998 by Mary Rice Hopkins

Published by Crossway Books
a division of Good News Publishers
1300 Crescent Street, Wheaton, Illinois 60187

Art Director: Brian Ondracek

Cover and Book Design: Cindy Kiple

First printing, 1998

Printed in Singapore

ISBN 1-58134-002-8

A NOTE FROM THE AUTHOR

Can you imagine how silly God's request of Noah may have seemed? Yet, after over 100 years of building, and people laughing at him, Noah never gave up or lost his trust in God. He was faithful. And even though Noah and his whole family were tossed about on the sea after following God's instructions, he still remained faithful.

What an important lesson to teach our children. As I cuddle up with my kids and read the story of Noah, I want them to know that God is faithful. In the storms of life, He is always there. While sometimes God's plans don't make sense to us at first, we can always trust that God knows best.

I hope you'll use the questions below to help secure these ideas in your children's minds once you've read the story together. If they come to believe God is faithful now—while they're young—they'll be able to trust Him in the future, no matter how severe the storm. Just like Noah. And that would be a faith worth having.

TO DISCUSS WITH YOUR CHILDREN

1. Noah was a friend of God. What does it mean to be God's friend?
    How can we get to know God?
2. In the story, Noah was found faithful. What does it mean to be faithful?
3. Noah and his family were on the boat for over a year. Each person had a chore to do such as feeding or cleaning up after the animals. How can you be helpful in your family?
4. Why did Noah want to follow God's directions? What might have happened if he didn't follow directions?
5. How does God still keep His promises today?

A voice said, "Noah, this is the Lord.
Build a big boat and climb aboard.
Soon it'll rain, then it will pour."
Noah was a faithful man.

So he built it wide, he built it long;

He built it high, he built it strong.

He followed God's plan so he couldn't go wrong.

Noah was a faithful man.

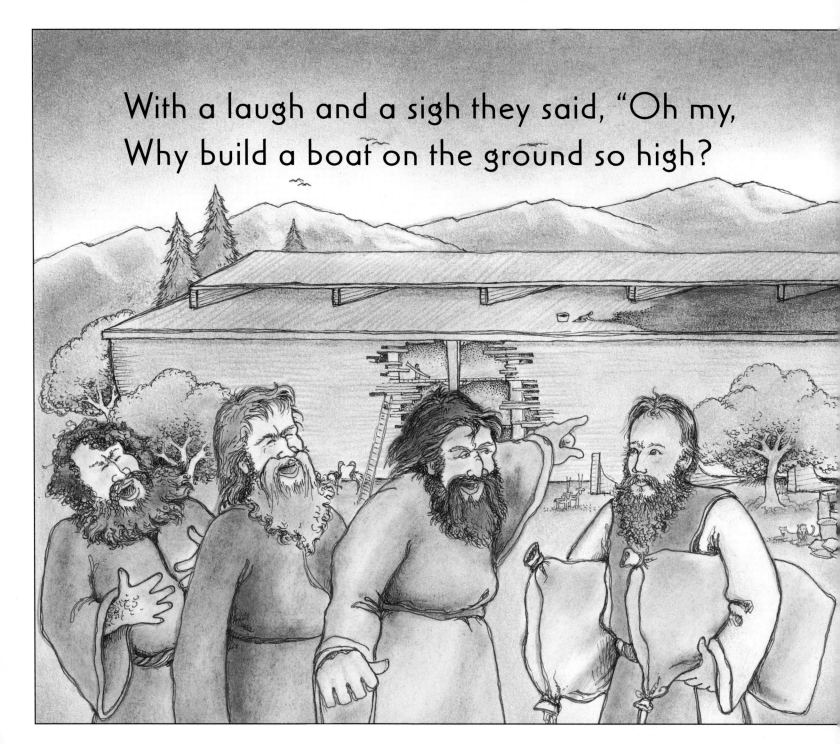

With a laugh and a sigh they said, "Oh my,
Why build a boat on the ground so high?

How can an ocean fall from the sky?"
But Noah was a faithful man.

The animals came two by two;
They hopped and galloped and crawled and flew—

The boat would a be a floating zoo.
Noah was a faithful man.

They all stepped up to the loading dock–
All of his family, herds and flocks.
God shut the door, they heard it lock.
Noah was a faithful man.

And it rained and it rained and it rained
Then it poured;
The oceans rose and the thunder roared.

Noah told the children to trust the Lord,
'Cause Noah was a faithful man.

For forty days the rain came down—
The water rose 'til it covered the ground.
There was only ocean all around,
But Noah was a faithful man.

Then the sun came out so warm, so grand;
Noah sent a dove to search for land.
She returned with an olive branch to his hand.
Noah was a faithful man.

It was over a year 'til the ark was parked—
To the roar of the lion and the song of the lark.
And all of the animals disembarked.
Noah was a faithful man.

A rainbow came, there was no more flood,
No more rain, no more mud.
Mrs. Noah gave her husband a great big hug,
'Cause Noah was a faithful man.

Yes it rained and it rained and it rained
Then it poured;
The oceans rose and the thunder roared.

Noah told the children to trust the Lord!
'Cause Noah was a faithful man.